Copyright © 2020 Dyan Richard

All rights reserved. No part of this publication may be reproduced, distributed, or transmitted in any form or by any means, including photocopying, recording, or other electronic or mechanical methods, without the prior written permission of the publisher, except in the case of brief quotations embodied in critical reviews and certain other noncommercial uses permitted by copyright law.

Table of Contents

INTRODUCTION

Sedentary lifestyle coupled with overeating are major causes of serious health conditions that are rampant in the 21st century. Due to the metamorphosis of technology in this century people tend to be less active, since technology aim at making life easier and stress free. Overeating and intake of junk foods are common in this century due to the availability and the fact that it is easy to get whenever hunger sets in, whereas all these habits are doing more harm than good to the body system. The liver is one of the major organ of the body that is responsible for hundreds of functions, one of its functions is in the process of digestion. When a lot of calories are consumed, the liver tends to work more and this can cause some damage to the liver.

One major condition that sets in is Non Alcoholic Fatty Liver Disease NAFLD. This is a type of liver disease that is not caused by ethanol use and it is characterised by fatty infiltration. Non-alcoholic fatty liver disease (NAFLD) is a major health problem because of its high prevalence and the associated risk of progression to liver cirrhosis, liver cancer and also, increased cardiovascular disease risks. Non alcoholic fatty liver disease (NAFLD) is caused by a build-up of fat in the liver in patients with little or no alcohol use. The exact cause of NAFLD is unknown, but it is usually associated with other medical issues like diabetes, obesity and high cholesterol.

Patients with NAFLD generally have high levels of the hormone insulin, but are resistant to some of the actions of insulin (insulin resistance). Both high levels of insulin and insulin resistance likely have a role in causing fat to accumulate in the liver. Fat build up in the liver can come from diet, increased fat production in the liver, or decreased ability of the liver to clear the fat. Genetics can affect all of these processes. Diets that contain high amounts of carbohydrates and sugars (including fructose and high fructose corn syrup) can stimulate fat production in the liver cells.

TYPES OF NAFLD

1. Nonalcoholic fatty liver (NAFLD) is when there is fat buildup in the liver without inflammation or damage to the liver cells. Fat accumulation without inflammation is called steatosis.
2. Nonalcoholic steatohepatitis (NASH) is when there is inflammation and liver cell injury associated with the buildup of fat.

Up to 30% of the US population, or about 80 million Americans, are estimated to have NAFLD! This rate is even higher in certain populations, such as Hispanics, Asians and Indians. NAFLD is the most common liver disorder in the United States and the rest of the developed world. As issues like obesity and diabetes are increasing in frequency, so is NAFLD. NAFLD is usually detected on imaging tests like ultrasound or CAT scans. Under the microscope, the liver structures are normal, but the liver cells have accumulations of fat in them.

RISK FACTORS FOR NAFLD

Patients with NAFLD tend to also have one or more features of the metabolic syndrome, but not always. Because of similar lifestyles and genetics, those with a family history of NAFLD may be at higher risk of developing this disease.

Metabolic Syndrome

Defined as having 3 or more of the following features:

- Obesity (BMI $\geq$30): particularly those with a large waist line or abdominal obesity, also known as being "apple shaped"
- Pre diabetes or diabetes*
- Low HDL cholesterol (low levels of good cholesterol)
- High lipids called triglycerides
- High blood pressure

SIGNS AND SYMPTOMS OF NAFLD

Patients with NAFLD/NASH typically have no symptoms or specific findings on physical exam.

Occasionally, patients will report vague discomfort in their right upper abdomen or fatigue. Abdominal imaging is often performed for other reasons and fatty liver is found incidentally. Liver tests can be completely normal.

DIAGNOSIS OF NAFLD

Diagnosis is not always simple because patients usually have no symptoms and liver tests can be completely normal. Even if they are elevated, liver tests alone cannot tell us how severe it is. Diagnosis is typically made if testing for other causes of liver disease is negative and there are characteristic findings of fat deposition on liver imaging tests (like ultrasound, CAT scan or MRI).

Liver biopsy is the only way to accurately differentiate between NAFLD and NASH. Biopsy can also determine the extent of the damage and measure the degree of fibrosis (scar tissue).

Noninvasive tests, like Fibroscan (transient elastography), can also estimate the amount of fat and scar tissue in the liver. Fibroscan is less accurate in severely obese persons, but it is a safe and simple test that can be repeated periodically to track liver damage over time.

TREATMENT OF NAFLD

Active research is ongoing, but for now there are no specific medications that can cure NAFLD. However, studies have shown that both fat, inflammation and scar tissue can leave your liver. This means that NAFLD and NASH can be reversible.

Lifestyle Modification

Improving liver fat and inflammation is possible when people lose weight and/or modify their lifestyle. This is the first line treatment for NAFLD. Lifestyle modification includes adopting a healthy diet as well as increasing physical activity. The goal is that these changes will become a permanent part of a daily routine and will be sustained for a lifetime.

• Losing 10% of your total current body weight increases the likelihood that the amount of liver fat and inflammation will improve. Weight loss should be gradual (a goal of 1-3 pounds per week), as rapid weight loss can actually worsen liver disease.

Medications: Vitamin E

Patients without diabetes and with NAFLD diagnosed with a liver biopsy will sometimes be asked to start Vitamin E (alpha-Tocopherol).

• Vitamin E is an antioxidant that is thought to help reduce liver inflammation.

• This medicine has not been studied in people with diabetes and is not safe to use with significant heart disease so do not start this medication without first talking with your liver doctor.

Managing other Diseases

• Improving control of other metabolic diseases such as diabetes, high blood pressure and high cholesterol/lipids can also help NAFLD.

Avoiding Alcohol

Moderate or heavy alcohol use can cause additional damage and fat accumulation in the liver in people with NAFLD. Therefore, patients with NAFLD should avoid alcohol entirely if possible. This will inhibit more damage in the liver.

Medication Safety in NAFLD

• Patients with cirrhosis must avoid pain medications called "non-steroidal anti-inflammatories (NSAIDS)". These include over-the-counter medications such as ibuprofen (Motrin®, Advil®), naproxen (Aleve® or Naprosyn®), as well as some prescription medications. Ask your doctor if any of your medications are NSAIDS.

• It is safe to use Tylenol® (acetaminophen) at doses of 2,000 mg/day or less (no more than 6 regular strength or no more than 4 extra strength tablets each day AND no more than 20 regular strength or no more than 15 extra strength tablets each week). Some cold medicines and prescription pain medicines contain acetaminophen, so read the labels and make sure you don't take too much by mistake.

• If otherwise indicated, statin medications are completely safe for patients with NAFLD/NASH, even for those with early cirrhosis.

Vaccinations

Those who are not immune to hepatitis A and B should undergo a vaccination series at 0, 1, and 6 months. This will prevent significant liver damage if exposed to either of these viruses.

The yearly influenza vaccination (flu shot) is also recommended.

PHYSICAL ACTIVITY RECOMMENDATIONS FOR PATIENTS WITH NAFLD

Being physically active is one of the best things you can do to get fit and stay healthy. Studies have shown that increases in physical activity can help decrease the amount of fat in your liver, particularly in patients who are able to lose 10% of their current body weight. Increasing your physical activity and improving your fitness is good for your heart, lungs, bones, muscles, and joints in addition to helping improve your liver health. Physical fitness lowers your risk for falls, heart attack, diabetes, high blood pressure, and some cancers. If you already have one or more of these problems, getting more fit may help you control other health problems and make you feel better. Being more fit also can help you to sleep better, handle stress better, and keep your mind sharp.

Key Points:

• Reduction of amount of fat in the liver results from an overall decrease in total calorie intake combined with an increase in physical activity.

• No one physical activity program has been proven to be more effective than another. Below are overall recommendations for increasing your physical activity level. What is most important is to find activities that work for you and that are able to do regularly.

• Even in the absence of significant weight loss, being more physically active has overall health benefits, including possibly decreasing the amount of fat in your liver.

WHAT IS PHYSICAL ACTIVITY & FITNESS?

Physical activity is any kind of activity that gets your body moving.

The types of physical activity that can help you get fit and stay healthy include:

• Aerobic or "cardio" activities: these activities make your heart beat faster and make you breathe harder. Examples include brisk walking, riding a bike, swimming or running. Aerobic activities strengthen your heart and lungs and build up your endurance.

• Strength/Resistance training activities: these activities make your muscles work against, or "resist," something and focus on building stronger muscles and bones. Examples include lifting weights, doing push-ups or using resistance bands.

• Stretching/flexibility activities: these activities work on flexibility and the ability to move your joints and muscles through their full range of motion. Stretching helps you be more flexible and avoid injury.

Fitness means being able to perform physical activity. It also means having the energy and strength to feel as good as possible. Getting more fit, even a little bit, can improve your health. You don't have to be an athlete to be fit. A brisk half-hour walk every day can help you reach a good level of fitness. And if this is hard for you, you can work toward a level of fitness that helps you feel better and have more energy.

HOW CAN YOU BE MORE PHYSICALLY ACTIVE?

Moderate physical activity is safe for most people. It is always a good idea to talk to your primary care doctor before becoming more active, especially if you haven't been very active or have health problems.

If you're ready to add more physical activity to your life, here are some tips to get you started:

• Make physical activity part of your regular day. Make a regular habit of using stairs, not elevators, and walking to do errands near your home.

• Start walking. Walking is a great fitness activity that most people can start doing. Make it a habit to take a daily walk with family members, friends, co-workers, or pets.

• Find an activity partner. This can make exercising more fun.

• Find an activity that you enjoy, and stay with it. Vary it with other activities so you don't get bored.

• Use Interactive Tools such as smart phone applications or pedometers/ activity trackers to monitor your physical activity level and find out how many calories you burn during exercise and daily activities.

HOW MUCH PHYSICAL ACTIVITY DO YOU NEED FOR HEALTH-RELATED FITNESS?

Experts say your goal should be one, or a combination, of these:

• Do some sort of moderate aerobic activity, like brisk walking, for at least 2½ hours each week. It is up to you how many days you want to exercise, but it is best to be active at least 3 days a week. Be active for at least 10 minutes at a time. For example, you could:

• Take a 10-minute walk 3 times a day. Do this 5 days a week.

• Take a half-hour walk 3 days a week. On the other 4 days take a 15-minute walk.

• Take a 45-minute walk every other day.

• Or do more vigorous activities, like running, for at least 1¼ hours a week. This activity makes you breathe harder and have a much faster heartbeat than when you are resting. You can spread out these

75 minutes any way you want to. It is better to be active at least 3 days a week for at least 10 minutes at a time. For example, you could:

- Run for 25 minutes 3 times a week.

- Run for 15 minutes 5 times a week.

Here's an easy way to tell if your exercise is moderate: You're at a moderate level of activity if you can talk but not sing during the activity. If you can't talk while you're doing the activity, you're working too hard.

HEALTHY WEIGHT

A healthy weight is a weight that lowers your risk for health problems. For most people, BMI (body mass index) and waist size are good ways to tell if they are at a healthy weight, although reaching a healthy weight isn't just about reaching a certain number. Speak to your doctor or nutritionist about what weight range is most appropriate for you. Patients who are able to lose 10% of their current body weight (through healthy eating and being physically active) have improvements in their liver health.

Fitness: Walking for Wellness

Walking is one of the easiest ways to get the exercise you need to stay healthy. Think of walking as an easy way to burn calories and stay fit while you go about your daily routine.

• Start with a short-term goal. For example, walk for 5 or 10 minutes every day. Or increase your number of steps by 300 to 500 each day.

• After you've made walking a habit, set a longer-term goal. You may want to set a goal of walking briskly for at least 30 minutes a day or work up to 10,000 steps a day. You can try to do this 5 days a week or more.

• You can use a phone app or wear a pedometer to track your steps each day. The first time you use it, count how many steps you normally take in a day. Track your activity every day, and set a goal for increasing the number of steps each day. At first, try to add 300 to 500 steps to your day. Then work toward 2,000 more steps a day. A good long-term goal is to get 10,000 steps a day.

• To stay motivated, find a walking partner, such as a family member, friend, or coworker. Daily dog walks are also a great way to keep up your walking routine.

• Try to incorporate more walking into your everyday activities. Add steps in whenever you can. Examples include:

• Taking the stairs instead of the elevator

• Parking further away in a parking lot to your destination.

• At work, get up and move around once an hour.

• When possible, walk to the grocery store, doctor appointments, work, school, or shopping. Walk a lap around the grocery store before you start shopping.

• Walk during TV commercials.

Safety Tips for Starting a Walking Program

- Know your surroundings. Walk in a well-lighted, safe place.
- Carry a cell phone for emergencies.
- Wear comfortable shoes and socks that cushion your feet.
- Pay attention to your walking surface. Use sidewalks and paths.
- If you usually walk outside and the weather is bad, take comfortable shoes to the mall and walk several laps inside.
- Drink plenty of water before, during, and after you are active. This is very important when it's hot outside and when you do intense exercise. Take a water bottle with you when you walk.

HEALTHY EATING RECOMMENDATIONS FOR PATIENTS WITH NAFLD

A healthy diet includes a variety of foods including fruits and vegetables, while limiting saturated fat, cholesterol, sugary foods and sodium. Healthy food habits can help reduce excess body weight. Studies have shown that a 10% reduction in body weight leads to significant improvement in the amount of fat in the liver.

You don't need to make huge changes to eat healthier and you don't have to change your habits all at the same time. It's best to set small goals and change your habits a little bit at a time. Over time, small changes can make a big difference in your health.

Key Points:

• Reduction of amount of fat in the liver results from an overall decrease in total calorie intake combined with an increase in physical activity.

• No one diet has been proven to be more effective than another. Below are overall recommendations for healthier eating habits. Focus first on identifying a few areas you might be able to improve on rather than trying to make all these changes at once.

• Limiting high fructose corn syrup and excess sugar may be a good place to start for many patients depending on your current eating habits.

• Even in the absence of significant weight loss, healthier eating has overall health benefits, including decreasing the amount of fat in your liver.

• For personalized recommendations, meeting with a nutritionist or dietician can provide more specific information for you.

GETTING STARTED ON A HEALTHY DIET

Watch Your Portions

• Did you know portion size and serving size are not the same thing? The National Institutes of Health provides helpful definitions of each:

Portion is how much food you choose to eat at one time, whether in a restaurant, from a package, or in your own kitchen. A portion is 100 percent under our control.

Serving Size is the amount of food listed on a product's Nutrition Facts label. All of the nutritional values you see on the label are for the serving size the manufacturer suggests on the package.

If you eat more than 1 serving (a bigger portion), you get more calories and nutrients. Being aware of the serving size can help you decide how much you want to eat of that food.

• Use tools! Measuring cups and spoons allow you to measure out exact portions of food at meals until you can estimate the right amount of food to serve yourself.

• You can also use a visual approach and divide your plate in to sections:

• Fill half of your meal plate with fruits and vegetables

• ¼ of your plate with a grain, preferably a whole grain like brown rice, whole wheat pasta

• ¼ with a protein source like lean meats, beans, tofu. Incorporate low fat dairy into your meals and or snacks

To keep your energy level up and keep you from feeling hungry, avoid skipping meals, which usually leads to overeating at the next meal. It is best to eat at regular intervals throughout the day such as 3 meals and 1 or 2 healthy snacks per day. Eat only the number of calories you need to stay at a healthy weight. If you need to lose weight, eat fewer calories than your body burns (through exercise and other physical activity). Try keeping a food log to see how many calories you are eating. The quality of calories is just as important as the quantity. A dietitian can advise you on a good calorie goal. Focus on the nutrient-dense foods listed below instead of highly processed snack foods, sugar-sweetened beverages, refined (white) grains, refined sugar, fried foods, foods high in saturated and trans fats.

Eat More Fruits and Vegetables

• Eat a variety of fruit and vegetables every day. Dark green, deep orange, red, or yellow fruits and vegetables are especially good for you. Examples include spinach, carrots, peaches, and berries.

• Aim for at least 5 (1/2 cup) servings of fruits and vegetables (combined) daily

• Keep fruits and vegetables handy for snacks. Store them where you can see it so that you will be tempted to eat it.

• Cook dishes that have a lot of veggies in them, such as stir-fries and soups.

Limit Sugar and Excess Carbohydrates

• Limit or avoid drinks and foods with added sugar. These include candy, desserts, and soda pop.

• High-Fructose Corn Syrup containing foods and beverages are particularly important to limit in order to promote weight loss and healthy eating.

• Although 100% fruit juices may not contain added sugar, fruit juice gives your body a large amount of sugar to process at one time and liquid calories are not as filling as whole foods. Choose a piece of fruit over juice. If you decide to drink juice, choose 100% and limit the amount to 4 ounces per day.

- Limiting the total amount of carbohydrates may be of benefit in NAFLD. On average, the total amount of carbohydrate for an adult ranges from 45-60 grams per meal. A standard serving size of carbohydrate food contains about 15 grams of carbohydrates.

- High carbohydrate foods include bread, cereal, rice, pasta, beans and starchy vegetables. Sweets tend to be high carbohydrate foods.

Completely Avoid Alcohol

- For your liver health we recommend completely avoiding alcohol intake. Alcohol intake when going through the healing or treatment process can cause many different health problems and can add excess calories that contribute to weight gain.

Limit Saturated and Trans Fat

Diets high in saturated fat increase bad cholesterol (LDL) and total cholesterol levels. Trans fats also raise LDL cholesterol.

Examples of Food High in Saturated Fat:

• Animal products: Fatty cuts of meat (beef, lamb, pork), Poultry with skin, Whole and 2% milk, Butter, Cheese, Lard

• Plant sources: Palm kernel oil, Palm oil, Coconut oil, Cocoa butter

Examples of Foods High in Trans Fat:

1. Baked goods (crackers, cookies, cakes, donuts)
2. Hard margarines
3. Commercially produced white breads
4. French fries and other fried foods
5. Trans fat is found in processed foods that use partially hydrogenated oils

Tips to Minimize Saturated and Trans Fat:

• Use olive or canola oil when you cook.

• Use Smart Balance or Earth balance spreads instead of butter or margarine

• Bake, broil, grill, or steam foods instead of frying them.

• Choose lean meats such as chicken or turkey breast, fish, eggs, and lean cuts of beef and pork like tenderloin or sirloin. When buying ground beef or turkey choose at least 90% lean/10% fat meats. Ground turkey can contain dark meat and skin so it's important to look for >90% lean turkey or ground turkey breast.

• Drain off any excess fat after cooking meats.

• Cut off all visible fat when you prepare meat and remove skin from chicken and turkey.

• Avoid high-fat meats such as hot dogs, salami, bologna, and sausages.

• Eat more plant-based proteins such as beans, lentils or soy as these have no saturated or trans fats. Soy products, such as tofu, edamame, and tempeh, may be especially good for you.

• Choose low-fat or fat-free milk and dairy products instead of whole-fat dairy or try unsweetened almond, soy, or cashew milk.

Limit Sodium

Almost all foods naturally contain sodium. Added salt in food preparation and food processing are the major sources of salt in our diet. Healthy adults require only 2400 milligrams sodium per day, yet the average American consumes 6000-8000 mg sodium daily. Limit how much salt and sodium you eat to help lower your blood pressure and reduce water retention.

Examples of Foods High in Salt/Sodium:

1. Cured meats, sausages, luncheon meats
2. Canned vegetables, soups, beans, fish
3. Soy sauce, miso
4. Commercially prepared main-course meals
5. Box dinners (seasoning packets)
6. Frozen meals
7. Cheeses, especially processed cheese

8. Condiments and other dressings: Mayonnaise, salad dressings, Ketchup, Sauces (barbecue, steak, Worcestershire)

Tips to Minimize Sodium:

• Taste food before salting. Add only a little salt when you think you need it. With time, your taste buds will adjust to less salt.

• Eat fewer snack items, fast foods, and other high-salt, processed foods. Check food labels for the amount of sodium in packaged foods.

• Choose low-sodium versions of canned goods (such as soups, vegetables, and beans).

• Use herbs and spices such as garlic, oregano, basil, onion, and pepper instead of salt.

• Use low sodium condiments whenever available such as ketchup, mustard, and salad dressings.

Eat Fish

• Eat at least two servings of fish a week.Certain fish, such as salmon and tuna, contain omega-3 fatty acids which may have health benefits.

Eat Foods High in Fiber

Fiber, in addition to lean protein, helps you feel fuller longer and may allow you to eat less calories each day.

• Choose whole-grain products. Examples include oats, whole wheat bread, quinoa, and brown rice.

• Buy whole-grain breads and cereals, instead of white bread or pastries.

• Fruits, vegetables, beans, nuts and seeds ae all good sources of fiber. Add walnuts or chia seeds to oatmeal or have almonds with a piece of fruit for an afternoon snack.

STRATEGIES FOR HEALTHY EATING

• Keep more fruits, low-fat dairy products (low-fat milk and low-fat yogurt), vegetables, and whole-grain foods at home and at work. Focus on adding healthy food to your diet, rather than just taking unhealthy foods away.

• Buy a healthy-recipe book, and cook more meals at home. Chew gum when you cook so you won't be tempted to snack on the ingredients.

• Pack a healthy lunch and snacks for work. This lets you have more control over what you eat.

• Limit eating out as much as possible. When you do eat out use above suggestions and split your meal or package half to take home for another meal.

• Put your snacks on a plate instead of eating from the package. This helps you control how much you eat.

• Don't skip or delay meals, and be sure to schedule your snacks. If you ignore your feelings of hunger, you may end up eating too much or choosing an unhealthy snack. If you often feel too hungry, it can cause you to focus a lot on food.

• Eat your meals with others when you can. Relax and enjoy your meals, and don't eat too fast. Try to make healthy eating a pleasure, not a chore.

• Drink water instead of high-sugar drinks (including high-sugar juice drinks). Sometimes dehydration can be confused with hunger. Aim to drink at least 6-8 cups of water daily.

• Try to substitute meatless main dishes 2-3 times per week. For example, use dried beans, split peas, lentils, soy and meat substitutes in place of meat in dishes.

• Use low fat frozen yogurt, sorbets, ice milk, etc as a dessert in place of ice cream.

• Bake, broil, and steam foods instead of frying them.

The Mediterranean diet features foods eaten in Greece, Spain, southern Italy and France, and other countries that border the Mediterranean Sea. It emphasizes eating a diet rich in fruits, vegetables, nuts, and high-fiber grains, and limits meat, cheese, and sweets.

This diet contains more fat than other healthy diets. But the fats are mainly from nuts, unsaturated oils, such as fish oils, olive oil, and certain nut or seed oils (such as canola, soybean, or flaxseed oil) that have been shown to have health benefits.

What to Eat

• Eat a variety of fruits and vegetables each day, such as grapes, blueberries, tomatoes, broccoli, peppers, figs, olives, spinach, eggplant, beans, lentils, and chickpeas.

• Eat a variety of whole-grain foods each day, such as oats, brown rice, and whole wheat bread, pasta, and couscous.

• Eat fish at least 2 times a week. Try tuna, salmon, mackerel, lake trout, herring, or sardines.

• Eat moderate amounts of low-fat dairy products each day or weekly, such as milk, cheese, or yogurt.

• Eat moderate amounts of poultry and eggs every 2 days or weekly.

• Choose healthy (unsaturated) fats, such as nuts, olive oil and certain nut or seed oils like canola, soybean, and flaxseed.

• Limit unhealthy (saturated) fats, such as butter, palm oil, and coconut oil. And limit fats found in animal products, such as meat and dairy products made with whole milk. Try to eat red meat only a few times a month in very small amounts.

• Limit sweets and desserts to only a few times a week. This includes sugar-sweetened drinks like soda.

Tips for Changing your Diet

• Dip bread in a mix of olive oil and fresh herbs instead of using butter.

• Add avocado slices to your sandwich instead of bacon.

• Have fish for lunch or dinner instead of red meat. Brush the fish with lemon and olive oil, and broil or grill it.

• Sprinkle your salad with seeds or nuts instead of cheese.

• Cook with olive or canola oil instead of butter or oils that are high in saturated fat.

• Switch from 2% milk or whole milk to 1% or fat-free milk.

• Dip raw vegetables in a vinaigrette dressing or hummus instead of dips made from mayonnaise or sour cream.

• Have a piece of fruit for dessert instead of a piece of cake. Try baked apples with cinnamon or strawberries topped with low fat Greek yogurt.

The following are the meals to be taken arranged in breakfast, lunch and snacks/dinner. All these meals are low in fat, sugar and sodium. Adhering strictly to the following coupled with consistence in the daily exercise routines will speed up recovering from NAFLD.

RECIPES

BREAKFAST

CREAMY OATS WITH CINNAMON AND BANANA

Serves 4

Ready In 15 min

Oats remain a healthy breakfast as it is high in fibre and is known to reduce cholesterol. Compared to boxed cereal, you can control the amount of salt and sugar when cooking oats. Serve it in different ways to keep it interesting. Try other spices like nutmeg or mixed spice with any seasonal fruit.

Ingredients

- 1 cup (250 ml) uncooked oats
- 1½ cups (375 ml) water
- 1½ cups (375 ml) low-fat milk
- ¼ tsp (1,2 ml) salt
- 1-2 bananas, sliced
- 1 tsp (5 ml) ground cinnamon

Directions

1. Place oats, water, milk and salt in a saucepan and bring to the boil over a medium heat. Once it starts to simmer, stir constantly to prevent lumps. Simmer for 5-10 minutes or until cooked.

2. Serve oats with banana and cinnamon.

TIPS

- Oats for one: ¼ cup (60 ml) uncooked oats with ¾ cup (180 ml) water (or half water and half low-fat milk) and a small pinch of salt. Prepare as explained, or mix in a big enough glass bowl and microwave for 3-5 minutes, depending on your microwave. Stir often and make sure it does not boil over.
- Pumpkin or sunflower seeds are delicious with oats and fruit. Try

chopped raw, unsalted almonds – use 30 ml (2 tbsp) per portion of oats.

- If you are used to sugar on your oats, try this version – the fruit adds a natural sweetness and you won't miss the sugar. If you struggle at first, gradually reduce the sugar until you don't need it at all anymore.

HOMEMADE MUESLI

Makes 1,2kg

Ready In 1hr

Making your own muesli is really easy and much more affordable than buying ready-made muesli. You can also control how much salt and oil is added.

Ingredients

- 1 kg (1 box) uncooked oats
- ½ cup (125 ml) raw almonds, chopped (optional)

- •   ½ cup (125 ml) sunflower seeds (optional)
- •   5 tbsp (75 ml) sunflower oil
- •   ¼ cup (60 ml) honey
- •   2 tsp (10 ml) vanilla essence

Directions

1. Preheat oven to 180 °C and line a baking tray with baking paper.
2. Place oats, nuts and seeds in a large mixing bowl. Place oil and honey in a separate bowl and melt in the microwave or a small saucepan over low heat for a few minutes. Stir in the vanilla.
3. Mix oil mixture well into oats mixture.
4. Spread oats in a single layer on the baking paper. Roast for 10 minutes. Stir through and roast for another 8-10 minutes or until golden brown and crispy.
5. Remove from the oven and allow to cool completely. Store in an airtight container for up to 4 weeks.

6. Serve ½ cup (125 ml) muesli per person with ¼ cup (60 ml) plain low-fat yoghurt and ½ cup (125 ml) of any fresh fruit. Add a pinch of cinnamon for more flavour.

TIPS

Use seasonal fruit like peaches, mangoes, grapes or berries in summer and pawpaw, banana, grapefruit, kiwi or naartjies in winter. Remember that ½ cup (125 ml) fruit is 1 portion.

BAKED BEANS ON TOAST

Serves 4

Ready In 20min

Baked beans and bread both contain salt already, so there is no need to add more to this dish. The lemon juice, black pepper, herbs and chutney adds a delicious flavour to this quick breakfast.

Ingredients

- 1 x 410 g tin baked beans in tomato sauce
- 2 tsp (10 ml) dried mixed herbs
- 2 tbsp (30 ml) chutney
- Lemon juice and black pepper to taste
- 4 slices wholewheat or brown bread, toasted
- 1 avocado, cubed (when in season)
- Fresh origanum leaves (optional)

Directions

1. Place beans, dried herbs and chutney in a saucepan. Bring to the boil over a medium heat. Reduce the heat and simmer until warmed through.

2. Season with lemon juice and pepper. Serve hot on toast with avocado and origanum.

TIPS

1. To add more flavour, season with paprika, any fresh herbs or even 2 tsp (10 ml) pesto. Fresh basil or thyme is delicious with beans. Stir in ½ tsp (2,5 ml) curry powder and 2 tsp (10 ml) chopped coriander for a spicier version.

2. For an even more filling breakfast, fry an egg in a little oil and serve on the beans or enjoy with a boiled egg. If preferred, serve beans only with the avocado.

3. Rye bread is also delicious with baked beans.

4. This is ideal as a light lunch or supper as well.

5. Try to choose a good quality chutney that is lower in added salt and sugar.

EGGS AND TOAST SOLDIERS

Serves 4

Ready In 30min

Sometimes a few simple ingredients can become a very healthy breakfast. Enjoy eggs with fresh ingredients and a slice of toast.

Ingredients

- 4 eggs

- 1 avocado, cut in slices (when in season)
- 2 tomatoes, cut in wedges
- ½ tsp (2,5 ml) salt
- lemon juice and black pepper to taste
- 4 slices wholewheat or brown bread, toasted

Directions

1. Place eggs with 1 cup (250 ml) water in a small saucepan and bring to a gentle simmer over a medium heat. Cover with a lid and simmer for 5-8 minutes, depending on how hard or soft you prefer the yolk to be. Cook for 5-7 minutes for soft yolks and 8-10 minutes for firm yolks.

2. Place eggs in egg cups and serve with slices of avocado and tomato. Lightly season avocado, tomato and egg with the salt and pepper. Add a squeeze of lemon juice to the avocado, if preferred.

3. Cut toast into thick strips to dunk into the egg or to spread with avocado.

TIPS

1. The avocado makes this dish more filling, which means you won't need more than one slice of toast. If you prefer, you can leave out the toast and just enjoy the fresh ingredients with the egg.
2. If you don't have time for eggs, spread toast with a thin layer of low-fat cottage cheese and serve with avocado and tomatoes.
3. This could also be served as a light meal with a salad.

FRESH FRUIT SALAD

Serves 5

Ready In 20min

It is important to eat seasonal fruit, as it will be more affordable and has much more flavour when in season. See what is available and choose a variety of colours to add lots of vitamins and minerals to your breakfast.

Ingredients

- Winter fruit salad
- 1 medium apple or pear
- 1 medium banana
- ½ medium pineapple
- 1 small grapefruit, orange or large naartjie
- ½ medium papaya
- Summer fruit salad
- 1 medium apple
- 1 medium banana
- ½ medium pineapple
- 1 medium peach or large apricot or plum
- 200 g berries, strawberries or grapes
- 1 small mango

To serve

- 300 ml plain low-fat yoghurt
- 150 ml sunflower seeds or chopped almonds

Directions

1. Prepare fruit by peeling, coring, slicing and chopping according to your choice of fruit. Mix together gently.

2. Serve 1 cup (250 ml) of fruit salad per person and add ¼ cup (60 ml) plain low-fat yoghurt and 2 tbsp (30 ml) sunflower seeds or almonds for a filling breakfast.

TIPS

1. Sprinkle with cinnamon or mint for a different flavour. Try to avoid adding honey, as the fruit is naturally sweet. Any nuts or seeds of your choice are delicious with this breakfast.

2. If preferred, serve fruit salad with ¼ cup (60 ml) homemade oats on page 22 for a more filling breakfast.

3. Enjoy ½ cup (125 ml) fruit salad as a snack portion between meals.

4. Did you know? One portion of whole fruit, the size of your fist = 1 portion of fruit; 1 cup (250 ml) of peeled and cut fruit for breakfast = 2 portions of fruit for the day.

5. Remember that lemon juice is a great seasoning when serving fruit. Add a few drops to 1 cup (250 ml) sliced fruit for extra flavour. This can also prevent the fruit from browning too quickly.

SUPER SMOOTHIE

Serves 4-5

Ready In 20min

A smoothie can be an interesting way to incorporate a variety of fruit into your breakfast. It's also quick and easy to enjoy – even on your way to work or school. By adding nuts or uncooked oats, you make the smoothie a bit more filling, which will keep you fuller for longer. Remember that a smoothie has to be nutritious otherwise it digests too fast – leaving you hungry sooner. A smoothie can also be part of a breakfast with a small portion of eggs or muesli and yoghurt.

Ingredients

- ½ medium papaya or 1 large mango, peeled and cubed
- 1 small banana, sliced
- 2 pears, plums, peaches or nectarines, cubed with the skin on
- ½ small pineapple, peeled and cubed
- ¼ cup (60 ml) uncooked oats or ground almonds (optional)

Ice cubes to serve

Directions

1. Place fruit in a blender or food processor and blend until smooth. Add oats or almonds, if preferred and blend for a few more minutes.
2. Place ice in tall glasses and pour smoothie into each glass. Thin down with a little water, yoghurt, rooibos tea or low-fat milk if too thick to your preference.

TIPS

1. When in season strawberries, grapes, mango and berries are delicious. Apples also work well.
2. A small glass of smoothie can also be enjoyed as a snack.
3. Add mint and a small piece of ginger to the fruit before blending for extra flavour.
4. Overripe fruit can be peeled, cut and frozen in freezer bags. Add this fruit to smoothies before blending for an ice cold treat.

WEEKEND OVEN-ROASTED VEGGIES

Serves 4

Ready In 1hr

This is a delicious, warm, vegetarian breakfast and the veggies are very versatile. See the tips below.

Ingredients

- 2 tbsp (30 ml) canola or olive oil

- 2 tbsp (30 ml) red wine or balsamic vinegar
- 1 tbsp (15 ml) dried mixed herbs
- ½ tsp (2,5 ml) salt
- Lemon juice and black pepper to taste
- 2 onions, cut in thin wedges
- 3 baby marrows, cut in thick slices
- 3 large tomatoes, cut in wedges
- 1 green or red pepper, cut in slices
- 3 large spinach leaves, shredded
- 4-8 eggs
- 4 slices wholewheat bread, toasted
- Large handful of fresh basil or parsley leaves (optional)
- 1 avocado, sliced (when in season)

Directions

1. Preheat oven to 200 °C. Mix oil, vinegar and dried herbs in a large bowl. Season with half the salt, lemon juice and pepper.

2. Add all the veggies, except the spinach and mix well to coat with the oil. Place in a single layer on a large baking tray.

3. Roast for 20 minutes or until the veggies are golden brown and cooked. Stir in spinach and roast for another 5 minutes to heat through.

4. Meanwhile, heat a very thin layer of oil in a frying pan. Fry eggs over a medium heat until cooked to your preference. Season with the remaining ¼ tsp (1,2 ml) salt.

5. Serve spoonfuls of veggies on toast. Place an egg (or 2 for a more filling breakfast or brunch) on top and season with pepper. Garnish with herbs and serve immediately with slices of avocado.

TIPS

1. Serve these veggies as a side dish with meat, fish or sausage or stir in a tin of chickpeas for a vegetarian meal. Left-overs are perfect for a lunch box.

2. If you enjoy an egg with a runny yolk, the yolk will be extra 'sauce' on the veggies.

3. Make a double batch of the veggies and use some for supper, tossed into pasta.

4. If you don't want to serve the veggies with eggs, heat a tin of pilchards in tomato sauce and serve on the veggies.

OMELETTE WITH BROCCOLI AND CHEESE

Serves 4

Ready In 30min

Ingredients

- 2 tbsp (30 ml) sunflower or canola oil
- 1 onion, sliced
- 100 g broccoli, cut in florets
- 1 tbsp (15 ml) dried mixed herbs
- Lemon juice and black pepper to taste
- 6 eggs, beaten
- ½ tsp (2,5 ml) salt
- ⅓ cup (80 ml) grated cheddar or mozzarella cheese

Directions

1. Heat half the oil in a frying pan over a medium heat and fry onion until soft.
2. Add broccoli and herbs and fry for a few more minutes until broccoli is just cooked, but still crunchy.
3. Season broccoli with a few drops of lemon juice and pepper.
4. Beat eggs and salt together. Add remaining oil to the veggies in the pan and stir through.
5. Pour eggs evenly over veggies, but don't stir. Reduce heat slightly.
6. Allow egg to set and lift cooked egg around the edges with an egg lifter, to allow raw egg to run in underneath. Continue this process until most of the egg has set, but don't stir the eggs. Sprinkle with cheese and allow to melt slightly.
7. Cover with a lid for a few minutes or until the egg is just set on top.
8. Serve with salad, slices of tomato or a slice of whole wheat toast. A dollop of chutney or sweet chilli sauce will also be delicious.

TIPS

1. Any veggies of your choice can be used for this omelette. If the veggies have lots of liquid, like mushrooms or tomatoes, first sauté them for a few minutes, like the broccoli in step 2, otherwise it could draw water once the egg is added.
2. Rocket leaves or spinach is also delicious with this omelette.
3. Substitute cheddar or mozzarella cheese with a slice of feta, if preferred.

EGG-IN-A-CUP

Serves 6

Ready In 40min

This is a quick, yet interesting way to serves eggs for breakfast or brunch. You can prepare the veggie filling or use left-over veggies. This recipe uses no salt, as the feta adds enough of a salty flavour.

Ingredients

- 2 tsp (10 ml) sunflower or olive oil
- 1 onion, chopped
- 2 baby marrows, thinly sliced
- 3 spinach leaves, shredded or sliced
- 1 tbsp (15 ml) dried origanum or 2 tbsp (30 ml) chopped fresh origanum
- 1 slice feta, crumbled
- Lemon juice and black pepper to taste
- 6 eggs

Directions

1. Heat oil over a medium heat in a small frying pan and fry onion and baby marrows until just soft.
2. Stir in spinach and herbs and fry until spinach has just wilted. Remove from the heat, stir in half of the feta and season to taste with lemon juice and pepper.
3. Divide mixture between 6 lightly greased, ovenproof cups or ramekins (ceramic bowls). Choose cups or bowls that will fit into a

saucepan or frying pan, so that it can be covered with a lid.

4. Bring 2-3 cm of water in the saucepan to a gentle simmer over medium heat.

5. Crack an egg into each cup, over veggies and sprinkle with remaining feta.

6. Carefully place cups in water in the saucepan or frying pan and fill with more boiling water if necessary, so that the cups stand halfway in water.

7. Cover with the lid and reduce the heat. Simmer gently for 8-10 minutes or until the egg yolks are cooked to your preference.

8. Serve with black pepper and salad ingredients or a slice of whole wheat toast per person. A small portion of fruit can also be served instead of the salad ingredients.

TIPS

1. Any left-over veggies, meat or chicken can be spooned into the bottom of the cups or bowls. Use about 80-100 ml of filling per cup.

2. Substitute the baby marrow for small broccoli florets or use 125 g mushrooms, sliced.

3. Left-over or tinned fish will also be delicious. Try tuna with the baby marrows or just spoon pilchards in tomato sauce into the bottom of the cups.

4. Prepare a light meal by using slightly bigger bowls and adding two eggs to each container.

EGGY TOAST

Serves 4

Ready In 45min

Eggy toast is an easy way to get kids to enjoy eggs if they don't like scrambled or fried eggs. Different toppings can be added for an interesting weekend breakfast or brunch idea.

Ingredients

- 4 eggs
- ¼ cup (60 ml) water
- ¼ tsp (1,2 ml) salt

- Black pepper to taste
- 1 tbsp (15 ml) sunflower or canola oil for frying
- 4 slices brown or whole wheat bread

Directions

To serve

- 2 pears, bananas or other fresh fruit, sliced
- 1 tsp (5 ml) honey per person
- Ground cinnamon

OR

- 1 tomato, sliced
- ½ cup (125 ml) grated cheddar or mozzarella cheese
- 1 tbsp (15 ml) chopped fresh herbs of your choice

Directions

1. Whisk eggs with water and season with salt and black pepper. Place in a shallow bowl.
2. Heat half of the oil over a medium heat in a frying pan.

3. Dip a slice of bread in the egg mixture and turn over with two forks to cover the bread completely with the egg mixture.

4. Fry 1–2 slices of bread on both sides until golden brown and repeat with the remaining bread and eggs. If the pan is big enough, all the slices can be fried together. If the pan is too small, don't dip the bread in the egg mixture too long in advance as it could become too soggy to handle and fry.

5. Remove bread from pan and keep warm, while frying the rest.

6. Serve with slices of fruit, drizzle with honey and sprinkle with cinnamon. Or serve with tomato and cheese and sprinkle with herbs.

TIPS

1. Serve a small portion of tinned fish on the toast for an even more filling breakfast.

2. If you are serving eggy toast with a savoury topping, add 1 tsp (5 ml) dried herbs of your choice to the egg mixture, before dipping the bread into it.

3. Slice 1 avocado to serve with the savoury options.

SPICY PAN BREAKFAST

Serves 6

Ready In 45min

Ingredients

- 5 tsp (25 ml) sunflower or canola oil
- 2 onions, halved and thinly sliced
- 1 clove of garlic, crushed
- 1 tbsp (15 ml) finely grated fresh ginger
- 1 carrot, grated
- 1 baby marrow, grated
- 1 tsp (5 ml) ground cumin
- 1 tsp (5 ml) ground coriander
- 1 tsp (5 ml) paprika or a pinch of cayenne pepper
- 1 chilli, seeded and chopped (optional)
- 1 x 410 g tin chopped tomatoes

- ½ tsp (2,5 ml) salt
- lemon juice and black pepper to taste
- 6 eggs
- 3 tbsp (45 ml) chopped fresh coriander or parsley

Directions

1. Heat half of the oil over a medium heat in a large frying pan. Fry onions, garlic and ginger until soft. Add carrot and baby marrow and fry for a few minutes.
2. Stir in the spices and chilli and fry until aromatic. Add tomatoes, reduce heat and simmer for 5 minutes. Season with salt, lemon juice and pepper.
3. Make 6 openings in the sauce and divide the rest of the oil between these openings.
4. Crack an egg into each opening and simmer with a lid for 4-5 minutes or until the yolks are cooked to your preference.
5. Sprinkle with fresh herbs and serve on toast or with slices of avocado.

TIPS

1. Other veggies like brinjals, baby marrows or mushrooms can be fried with the onions.
2. Add a tin of beans to the sauce, before adding the eggs, to make this an even more filling breakfast or light meal.

VERSATILE SCRAMBLED EGGS

Serves 4-6

Ready In 20min

Ingredients

- 8 eggs
- ½ cup (125 ml) water
- ½ tsp (2,5 ml) salt
- black pepper to taste
- 2 tsp (10 ml) sunflower or olive oil
- 3 tbsp (45 ml) fresh herbs of your choice, like origanum, parsley, dill or thyme

You can add 1 of any of the following:

- ½ cup (125 ml) grated cheddar or mozzarella cheese
- 1 slice feta, crumbled
- 1 x 170 g tuna in water, drained
- ½ cup (125 ml) frozen peas or whole kernel corn, rinsed and patted dry
- 125 g mushrooms, sliced and pan-fried in a very small amount of oil

Directions

1. Beat eggs with water, salt and pepper in a bowl.
2. Heat oil in a frying pan over medium heat and add the egg mixture.
3. Allow egg to start setting before stirring too much. Then gently stir egg with an egg lifter, to ensure that all the raw egg is cooked. Don't over-mix the eggs and don't make the pan too hot, otherwise the eggs can separate quite easily. Reduce heat if necessary.
4. If you want to add another ingredient from the list above, add this after stirring the eggs for the first time.

5. Gently stir scrambled eggs until just cooked and serve immediately. Sprinkle with herbs and black pepper and serve with a slice of wholewheat or brown toast per person and tomato slices, if preferred.

TIPS

1. For a delicious, yet easy seasoning, stir the chopped herbs into the egg mixture, before adding it to the pan.

LUNCH

MINI MEAT BALLS

Serves 4

Ready In 45min

Ingredients

- 500 g lean beef mince
- 2 tbsp (30 ml) chutney
- 2 tbsp (30 ml) tomato sauce
- 2 baby marrows, grated

- ¼ cup (60 ml) uncooked oats
- 1 egg, beaten
- 2 tsp (10 ml) dried mixed herbs
- 1 tbsp (15 ml) ground coriander
- 3 tbsp (45 ml) chopped fresh parsley
- ½ tsp (2,5 ml) salt
- Lemon juice and black pepper to taste
- 2 tbsp (30 ml) sunflower or canola oil for frying

Directions

1. Place all the ingredients, except the oil, in a mixing bowl and mix with your hands until well combined. Season with lemon juice and pepper.
2. Shape the mince mixture into small balls using about 2 tbsp (30 ml) of mince per ball.
3. Heat half of the oil in a large frying pan over a medium heat. Fry half of the meat balls until golden brown on both sides.
4. Reduce the heat, cover with a lid and simmer for a few minutes or until cooked. Spoon out and repeat with remaining meat balls and oil.

5. Allow meat balls to cool and pack in a lunch box with a dipping sauce of your choice, such as sweet chilli sauce, tomato sauce or plain low-fat yoghurt. Alternatively serve warm with salad ingredients as a light lunch.

TIPS

1. When buying sauces like chutney and tomato sauce, make sure you choose a good quality option that is lower in sugar and salt. Check the food labels and see page 12 for more on reading food labels.

2. The meat balls can also be served with fresh fruit or left-over cooked veggies like sweet potato, butternut or even corn on the cob. Baby potatoes in the skin also work well. The meatballs are delicious as a filling for pitas with salad ingredients.

3. This recipe makes about 12-15 small meat balls.

SPICY BUTTER BEAN BITES

Serves 4

Ready In 45min

These vegetarian bites are packed with flavour and delicious on their own or as part of a lunch box. See the serving ideas below and assemble at work when you are ready to eat it.

Ingredients

- 1 x 410 g tin butter beans, drained and rinsed
- 1 small onion, grated
- 2 tsp (10 ml) grated lemon rind
- 2 tbsp (30 ml) lemon juice
- 2 tsp (10 ml) ground cumin
- 2 tsp (10 ml) ground coriander
- ½-1 tsp (2,5-5 ml) mild curry powder
- 3 tbsp (45 ml) chopped fresh parsley or coriander
- 1 tbsp (15 ml) dried origanum
- 2 tbsp (30 ml) wholewheat flour
- 1 egg, beaten
- ¼ tsp (1,2 ml) salt

- Black pepper to taste
- 2 tbsp (30 ml) sunflower or olive oil for frying

Directions

1. Place all the ingredients, except the oil, in a mixing bowl. Mash with a fork or a potato masher until smoother. Season with pepper and more lemon juice if preferred.

2. Heat half of the oil in a large frying pan over a medium heat. Drop spoonful of the mixture into the pan and fry until golden. Don't press down on the mixture so that they keep their shape.

3. Turn over as the mixture starts to set and fry for a few more minutes. Reduce heat and cover with a lid to allow to cook through for a 1-2 minutes. Spoon out and repeat with remaining mixture and oil.

4. Serve bites as part of a lunch box with lemon wedges and fresh fruit or veggies. They are delicious in a whole wheat pita or wrap with low-fat yoghurt and a salsa made with cucumber, tomato and red and yellow peppers.

They are equally yummy hot or at room temperature.

TIPS

1. If the curry flavour is too strong for your kids, substitute the curry powder with dried mixed herbs.
2. Make a double batch of this recipe and keep for lunch boxes or as snacks for up to 3 days.
3. This recipe makes 15 bites.

TUNA AND CORN CAKES

Serves 4

Ready In 45min

These easy and tasty little fish cakes are perfect to get kids to eat more veggies – especially at lunchtime. You could add different flavours or spices to the mixture, such as paprika or dried mixed herbs. For a spicier flavour add a pinch of cayenne pepper.

Ingredients

- 1 x 170 g tin tuna in water, drained
- 1 x 410 g tin cream style sweetcorn
- ⅓ cup (80 ml) frozen peas, rinsed
- 1 cup (250 ml) wholewheat flour
- ½ tsp (2,5 ml) baking powder
- 2 eggs, beaten
- 2 tbsp (30 ml) chopped fresh parsley
- ¼ tsp (1,2 ml) salt
- 1 tbsp (15 ml) lemon juice
- Black pepper to taste
- 2 tbsp (30 ml) sunflower or canola oil for frying

Directions

1. Place all the ingredients, except the oil, in a large mixing bowl. Mix until well combined.
2. Heat half of the oil in a large frying pan over a medium heat. Fry small spoonfuls of the mixture on both sides until golden brown and cooked.
3. Spoon out and drain on paper towel. Repeat with the rest of the mixture and a little extra oil if necessary.

4. Serve as part of a lunch box with lemon wedges, sweet chilli sauce, tomato sauce or chutney. Carrot sticks, blanched broccoli florets and wedges of fruit like apple and pear will make for a more filling lunch.

TIPS

1. If preferred, use pilchards in tomato sauce instead of the tuna. Drain the tomato sauce and freeze to add as a liquid to fish soup or stew. Left-over cooked fish also works well.
2. If your kids enjoy frozen veggies, add any other frozen veggie, like more corn or carrots to the mixture.

CREAMY FISH SPREAD

Serves 6

Ready In 20min

A versatile spread to enjoy with veggies, on bread or in a sandwich.

Ingredients

- 1 x 420 g tin pilchards in tomato sauce, drained, but keep the sauce
- 125 g plain low-fat cottage cheese
- Pinch of cayenne pepper
- 2 tbsp (30 ml) dried origanum
- 2 tbsp (30 ml) lemon juice
- Black pepper to taste

Directions

1. Place fish in a large bowl and mash with a fork until fine. Stir in the remaining ingredients and season to taste with pepper. Add some of the drained tomato sauce to taste, but take care not to add too much as it may become too runny.
2. Spread on 2 slices of whole wheat or brown bread. Add avocado when in season or tomato and lettuce for a tasty sandwich. Serve with fresh fruit, if preferred. It is also great as a dip with veggies.

TIPS

1. Place the spread in an airtight container and store in the fridge for up to 3 days.

2. If preferred, blend the mixture with a stick blender for a smoother spread.

3. If there is any left-over tomato sauce from the tin, it can be frozen and added to any tomato and fish dish, such as a pasta sauce, for extra flavour.

VEGETARIAN CHICKPEA SALAD

Serves 4

Ready In 30min

Ingredients

- 2 medium tomatoes, cubed
- ¼ cucumber, cubed
- 2 medium carrots, quatered and sliced
- 1 slice feta, cubed
- 2 x 410 g tin chickpeas or beans of your choice, drained and rinsed

- 1 avocado, cubed (when in season)

Salad dressing

- 1 tbsp (15 ml) red or white grape vinegar
- 2 tbsp (30 ml) canola or olive oil
- 1 tsp (5 ml) dried or 2 tsp (10 ml) fresh thyme leaves
- ½ tsp (2,5 ml) ground cumin
- ½ tsp (2,5 ml) sugar
- ¼ tsp (1,2 ml) salt
- Lemon juice and black pepper to taste

Directions

1. Mix all the salad ingredients together.
2. Salad dressing: Mix all the ingredients together and season with lemon juice and pepper.
3. Toss dressing through the salad. Keep the avocado separate and cut just before eating. Enjoy as a light meal or as lunch at work. Pack a portion of fruit for a more filling lunch.

TIPS

1. For a different flavour, use orange juice instead of the vinegar in the salad dressing. Leave out the sugar.
2. This salad will be delicious with herbs like mint and parsley. Add fresh leaves to the salad just before serving.
3. Beans like red kidney beans, butter beans and cannellini beans work well in this dish. Use a combination of beans and chickpeas or just beans, if preferred.

GREEN SALAD WITH CHICKEN

Serves 4-6

Ready In 1hr

Ingredients

Chicken

- 1 tsp (5 ml) sunflower or olive oil
- 2 chicken breasts on the bone, skin removed
- ⅓ cup (80 ml) rooibos tea

- 1 bay leaf

  Salad

- ½ tbsp (7,5 ml) prepared mild mustard
- 3 tbsp (45 ml) lemon juice or white grape vinegar
- 1 tsp (5 ml) sugar or honey
- 3 tbsp (45 ml) sunflower or olive oil
- ½ tsp (2,5 ml) dried origanum
- Black pepper to taste
- 100 g broccoli, cut in florets or thin green beans, halved
- 1 cup (250 ml) frozen peas, rinsed
- ¼ cucumber, halved and sliced
- Large handful mixed lettuce leaves

Directions

1. Chicken: Heat the oil in a large frying pan over a medium heat and fry chicken on both sides until golden brown.

2. Reduce heat, add tea and bay leaf. Cover with a lid. Simmer for 20-25 minutes or until just cooked. Spoon out and allow to cool. (Freeze the pan juices and use as a stock for another

meal.) Remove the bones from the chicken and shred the meat.

3. Salad: Mix mustard, lemon juice, sugar, oil and origanum and season with pepper. Pour some of this mixture over the chicken to marinade the cooked meat.

4. Pour boiling water over the broccoli or beans and peas. Allow to stand for 7-10 minutes or until cooked. Drain and repeat if necessary. Rinse well to cool.

5. Toss the cooked veggies and chicken with cucumber and lettuce and serve with the remaining dressing. If you are packing into a lunch box, keep the lettuce and extra salad dressing separate until you are ready to eat. Enjoy with left-over cooked veggies such as butternut, sweet potato or corn or a slice of whole wheat bread.

TIPS

1. Although dried herbs are convenient, fresh herbs like origanum, rosemary and thyme will be delicious in this salad.

2. Use this method to cook chicken for any dish. It is easy and the chicken stays juicy.

CRISPY CHICKEN STRIPS

Serves 4

Ready In 45min

Chicken nuggets or crumbed chicken is a firm favourite, but unfortunately often unhealthy as it is deep-fried. These chicken strips are coated in polenta or mealie meal which adds an extra crunch and are fried in a small amount of oil.

Ingredients

- 1 cup (250 ml) uncooked fine polenta or mealie meal
- 3 tbsp (45 ml) dried mixed herbs
- ½ tsp (2,5 ml) salt
- Black pepper to taste
- 4 chicken breast fillets, cut into thin strips
- 1 cup (250 ml) buttermilk
- 3 tbsp (45 ml) sunflower or olive oil for frying

Directions

1. Mix polenta or mealie meal, dried herbs and salt in a large, shallow dish and season to taste with pepper.

2. Dip a few chicken strips at a time into the buttermilk and roll in the polenta mixture to coat each strip. (Work with two forks to stop your hands from getting too messy.)

3. Heat 1 tbsp (15 ml) of the oil in a large frying pan over a medium heat. Fry chicken strips in batches, until just golden brown on both sides and cooked. The thin strips fry quickly, so don't overcook them, as the chicken will become dry. Repeat with the rest of the chicken and oil.

4. Serve hot or at room temperature with lemon wedges and a sauce of your choice, such as a sweet chilli sauce. Enjoy chicken strips with salad ingredients, fresh fruit or left-over veggies like butternut.

TIPS

1. Omit the buttermilk and lightly brush each chicken strip with a little extra oil and then coat and fry as above.
2. Try this recipe with any firm line fish.
3. for a delicious sauce to serve with your chicken strips, season mayonnaise or plain low-fat yoghurt with a little lemon juice.

CRUNCHY LENTIL SALAD

Serves 4

Ready In 45min

Ingredients

- 1 cup (250 ml) uncooked brown lentils
- ½ tsp (2,5 ml) salt
- 2 tsp (10 ml) dried origanum
- 2 tbsp (30 ml) sunflower or olive oil
- 1 tbsp (15 ml) red wine vinegar
- ½ tsp (2,5 ml) sugar

- Black pepper to taste
- 3 tbsp (45 ml) fresh chopped parsley
- 3 medium carrots, coarsely grated
- 2 tomatoes, halved and sliced
- 3 large spinach leaves, shredded

Directions

1. Place lentils, half the salt and half the origanum with 3 cups (750 ml) water in a pot. Bring to the boil over a medium heat. Reduce the heat and simmer for 20-30 minutes or until just cooked.
2. Drain lentils, rinse with cold water and drain well.
3. Meanwhile, make the salad dressing. Mix remaining salt and origanum with the oil, vinegar and sugar and season with pepper.
4. Add the rest of the ingredients to the cold lentils and mix well. Add the dressing just before serving. Pack with some extra fruit for a filling meal.

TIPS

1. This salad will also be perfect for a side dish at a braai.

2. Avocado will be great in this salad. When in season, cut in cubes and add at the end.

ROASTED CHICKPEA DIP

Serves 6-8

Ready In 45min

A chickpea dip, also known as hummus, is traditionally made with tahini which is a sesame seed paste. Tahini however can be expensive or difficult to find. By roasting half of the chickpeas with cumin seeds before blending them, the hummus still has a nutty flavour.

Ingredients

- 2 x 410 g tins chickpeas, drained, but keep the liquid
- 2 large cloves of garlic, crushed
- 5 tbsp (75 ml) sunflower or olive oil

- 1 tsp (5 ml) cumin seeds
- 1 tsp (5 ml) ground cumin
- 100 ml lemon juice
- ¼ tsp (1,2 ml) salt
- Black pepper to taste

Directions

1. Preheat the oven to 180 °C and line a small baking tray with foil. Pat chickpeas dry with paper towel. Place 1 of the tins of chickpeas with the garlic, 30 ml (2 tbsp) of the oil and cumin seeds in a large bowl and mix to coat the chickpeas.
2. Place the oil-coated chickpeas with the seasonings on the baking tray and roast for 15-20 minutes or until lightly golden brown.
3. Place roasted chickpeas with the oil and seasonings from the tray, in a large bowl. Add the remaining chickpeas, oil, ground cumin and lemon juice. Add 50 ml of the reserved liquid from the tin. Blend to form a chunky mixture and season to taste. Add more water, if you prefer a smoother dip.

4. Serve as part of a lunch with fresh veggies like carrots, celery, cucumber and green beans. It is also delicious spread onto bread, any sandwich or as a dip for whole wheat pita wedges.

TIPS

1. Refrigerate dip in an airtight container for 4-5 days.
2. If preferred, stir in a little plain low-fat yoghurt for a creamier dip.

QUICK VEGGIE SOUP

Serves 6

Ready In 1hr

Make a big batch of this soup and freeze in lunch-sized portions for work. It is also perfect as a light supper – keep any left-overs for lunch.

Ingredients

- 1 tbsp (15 ml) sunflower or olive oil

- 1 onion, finely chopped
- 2 celery stalks, chopped
- 2 baby marrows, chopped
- 1 medium sweet potato with the skin, grated
- 4 cups (1 litre) water
- 1 x 410 g tin butter beans, drained and rinsed
- ½ tsp (2,5 ml) salt
- 1 tsp (5 ml) dried thyme
- 100 g broccoli, cut in florets
- 2 spinach leaves, shredded
- 1 tsp (5 ml) prepared mild mustard
- lemon juice and black pepper to taste
- 2 tbsp (30 ml) chopped fresh parsley (optional)

Directions

1. Heat oil in a large pot over a medium heat. Fry onion until soft and add celery and baby marrows. Fry for a few more minutes and add sweet potato, water, beans, salt and thyme.
2. Cover with a lid and simmer for 15-20 minutes or until the sweet potato is cooked.
3. Add broccoli, spinach and mustard and season with lemon juice and pepper. Simmer for

another 10 minutes or until the broccoli is just cooked. Blend until smooth or mash with a potato masher for a chunkier soup. Season with lemon juice and pepper.

4. Stir in the parsley and serve hot. See tips for serving ideas.

TIPS

1. Serve soup with a dollop of plain low-fat yoghurt, more fresh herbs or a few drops of olive oil.

2. Season the soup to your preference with spices like paprika, cumin, garam masala or curry powder.

3. Left-over chicken or fish can be stirred into soup to make it more filling. Any other tinned or cooked beans can be added.

GUACAMOLE

Serves 4-6

Ready In 15min

Ingredients

- 2 ripe avocados, mashed with a fork or cubed
- 1 tbsp (15 ml) lemon juice
- ½ tsp (2,5 ml) finely grated lemon rind
- 5 ml (1 tsp) ground cumin
- 3 tbsp (45 ml) chopped fresh parsley or coriander
- 1 small ripe tomato, chopped
- ¼ tsp (1,2 ml) salt
- Black pepper to taste

Directions

1. Mix avocados, lemon juice, lemon rind, cumin, herbs and tomato. Add salt and season with pepper.
2. Serve as part of a light lunch as a dip with fresh veggies like cucumber, peppers or carrot sticks. Dip toasted whole wheat pitas into the guacamole or spread onto any sandwich. Enjoy with fresh fruit and a handful of nuts or seeds.

TIPS

1. Add paprika, cayenne pepper or chilli to the guacamole for a spicier flavour.

2. Grating lemon rind is easy, just use the small side of the grater and don't grate any of the bitter, white pith.

3. This guacamole is not only great as part of a lunch, but equally good with meat, fish or chicken. Serve it on wholewheat toast or a sandwich for a quick lunch.

4. Stir chopped onion or spring onions into the mixture for added flavour. Alternatively stir plain low-fat yoghurt into the guacamole to use as a dip.

LIGHTLY ROASTED NUTS

Serves 6

Ready In 30min

These nuts are a great alternative to salty shop-bought versions.

Ingredients

- 200 g raw unsalted nuts, like almonds or peanuts
- 1 tbsp (15 ml) canola or olive oil
- 1 tsp (5 ml) paprika
- ½ tsp (2,5 ml) ground cumin
- ½ tsp (2,5 ml) ground cinnamon
- Black pepper to taste

Directions

1. Preheat the oven to 180 °C and line a baking tray with baking paper or foil.

2. Place all the ingredients in a mixing bowl and stir well to coat the nuts in the oil and spices. Season with pepper.

TIPS

1. Choose a combination of nuts and seeds like sunflower seeds, pumpkin seeds, pecan nuts, peanuts and almonds.
2. Store these nuts in an airtight container for about 1 week.
3. Make a sweeter flavour combination. Substitute spices for 1 tsp (5 ml) ground cinnamon, ½ tsp (2,5 ml) ground mixed spice and a pinch of nutmeg. Omit the pepper. Enjoy as a snack or sprinkle over oats or fruit salad for breakfast.
4. Combine the nuts with dried fruit like raisins or cranberries or eat with fresh fruit for a healthy snack.
5. Make these nuts on the stove. Heat oil in the pan and add nuts. Fry until lightly golden brown. Add spices and fry for a few more minutes.

RAISIN COOKIES

Makes 25-30

Ready In 45min

Homemade cookies are much better than shop-bought cookies, because you can control what goes into them. These are lower in fat and sugar, making them a healthier alternative.

Ingredients

- ⅓ cup (80 ml) soft tub margarine
- ⅓ cup (80 ml) sugar
- 2 eggs, beaten
- 1 tsp (5 ml) vanilla essence
- 1 tsp (5 ml) finely grated lemon rind
- 1 cup (250 ml) wholewheat flour
- 1 cup (250 ml) cake flour
- 100 ml raisins

Directions

1. Preheat the oven to 180 °C and line a baking tray with baking paper.

2. Place margarine and sugar in a mixing bowl and beat until light and fluffy.

3. Add eggs one at a time, beating well after each addition.

4. Stir in the vanilla and lemon rind and fold in both of the flours and raisins. Stir to form a smooth dough. Roll into balls and place on the baking tray. Press down with a fork.

5. Bake for 15 minutes or until golden brown. Cool on a cooling rack and store in an airtight container. Serve 2-3 small cookies as a snack.

TIPS

1. Use this cookie dough as a base for any cookie. Stir in chocolate chips for a special occasion.

2. Add ½ tsp (2,5 ml) ground ginger and 1 tsp (5 ml) ground mixed spice to the dough for a spiced cookie.

PEANUT BUTTER SLICES

Serves 20

Ready In 40min

Peanut butter is a wonderful baking ingredient. Here is helps to bind the mixture and adds flavour.

Ingredients

- 2 cups (500 ml) oats
- ⅓ cup (80 ml) honey
- ⅓ cup (80 ml) pitted dates, chopped
- 5 tbsp (75 ml) peanut butter
- 1 egg, beaten
- ¼ cup (60 ml) sunflower oil
- 1 tsp (5 ml) ground cinnamon or mixed spice
- 1 tsp (5 ml) vanilla essence

Directions

1. Preheat the oven to 180 °C and lightly grease an 18 x 30 cm baking tin.

2. Place all the ingredients in a mixing bowl and mix until well combined.

3. Press mixture into the baking tin in an even layer and bake for 10-15 minutes or until golden brown and crispy.

4. Cut into 20 slices while they are still slightly warm. Allow to cool on a cooling rack and remove from the tin. Store in an airtight container for 3-4 days.

5. Serve 2 slices per person as a snack.

TIPS

1. If pitted dates aren't available, you can use raisins or dried cranberries.
2. Make sure you choose a good quality peanut butter that is lower in salt and sugar. Check the food labels and see page 12 for more detail on reading food labels.

DATE AND CHOCOLATE BALLS

Makes 20

Ready In 30min

We all love chocolate, but know that too much is not good for us. In this treat, we combine dark chocolate with dates to make a healthier alternative.

Ingredients

- ½ x 80 g slab dark chocolate, broken into pieces
- 1 tbsp (15 ml) cocoa
- 3 tbsp (45 ml) low-fat milk
- 1 tsp (5 ml) vanilla essence
- 250 g pitted dates, finely chopped
- 100 ml desiccated coconut
- Extra coconut and cocoa to decorate with

Directions

1. Place chocolate in a glass bowl and melt over gently simmering water. Make sure that the bowl does not touch the water.

2. Mix cocoa with some of the milk to form a paste and mix with remaining milk and vanilla. Stir some of the melted chocolate into the milk mixture until smooth. Mix into the warm chocolate.

3. Stir in dates and coconut. Place spoonful of the mixture onto baking paper and sprinkle with coconut or cocoa and allow to set. Alternatively allow to cool slightly and then roll into balls. Roll balls into extra coconut or cocoa, if preferred. Allow to cool in the fridge. Serve 1–2 balls as a treat.

TIPS

1. Serve date balls as part of a dessert with fresh fruit or serve with coffee at the end of a meal.

2. If packing for a lunch box treat, make sure that it is kept in a cool place, as they may melt.

3. Choose a good quality chocolate and cocoa that is low in added sugar. Check your food labels to make better choices and see page 12 for more detail.

BABY MARROW FRITTERS

Makes 25

Ready In 45min

Baby marrows are very versatile and add extra fibre and flavour to this snack.

Ingredients

- 1½ cups (375 ml) wholewheat flour
- 1 tsp (5 ml) baking powder
- 1 cup (250 ml) buttermilk or maas
- 2 eggs, beaten
- 4 baby marrows, coarsely grated
- 6 tbsp (90 ml) grated cheddar or mozzarella cheese
- 2 tbsp (30 ml) sunflower or olive oil for frying

Directions

1. Place dry ingredients in a large mixing bowl. Beat buttermilk and eggs together in a separate bowl. Stir buttermilk mixture into the dry mixture until well combined.

2. Stir in the baby marrows and cheese and mix to form a thick batter.

3. Heat half of the oil in a large frying pan and fry spoonful of the mixture until golden brown. Turn over and fry on the other side until golden brown and cooked. Drain on paper towel.

4. Repeat with remaining mixture and more oil if necessary. Serve 3 fritters per person as a snack.

TIPS

1. Add a pinch of paprika to the batter, if preferred.

2. Add chopped fresh origanum, thyme or even parsley to the mixture.

3. Serve these fritters as a snack before a braai instead of crisps.

HOMEMADE ICE TEA

Serves 6

Ready In 2hrs 30min

This tea is very refreshing and a healthier alternative to fizzy, sugary cold drinks. Keep a jug of this ice tea in the fridge in summer.

Ingredients

- 8 rooibos tea bags
- 1 cinnamon stick
- 4 whole cloves
- 6 thin slices ginger
- 4 cups (1 litre) boiling water
- 4 cups (1 litre) 100 % grape, apple or berry juice, chilled
- Lemon juice to taste
- Ice cubes, mint leaves, fresh fruit or lemon slices to serve

Directions

1. Place tea bags, spices and ginger in a large glass jug and pour over boiling water. Stir well

and allow to cool for about 2 hours. Remove tea bags, ginger and spices.

2. Add juice to the tea and season with lemon juice to taste.

3. Serve ice cold with ice and your choice of mint leaves, fruit and lemon.

TIPS

1. When buying fruit juice, remember to read the label and only buy pure or 100 % fruit juice.

2. In summer when it's hot outside, freeze this ice tea in ice cube or ice lolly trays for the kids. This is a good alternative to ice-cream. * Includes cooling time

APPLE AND BANANA MUFFINS

Makes 10-12

Ready In 1hr 30min

Baking is often associated with lots of sugar and a lower nutritional value. By preparing an apple purée and using a ripe banana, no sugar is needed.

Grated apple adds flavour and texture to these delicious muffins.

Ingredients

- Apple purée (makes 250 ml)
- 4 apples, peeled and cubed
- ¼ cup (60 ml) water
- 2 tsp (10 ml) lemon juice
- Muffins
- ½ cup (125 ml) wholewheat flour
- ½ cup (125 ml) cake flour
- ½ tbsp (7,5 ml) baking powder
- 1 tsp (5 ml) ground cinnamon
- 1 cup (250 ml) coarsely grated apple
- ½ cup (125 ml) prepared apple purée
- 1 large ripe banana, mashed with a fork
- 2 eggs, beaten
- 6 tbsp (90 ml) sunflower or canola oil
- 1 tsp (5 ml) vanilla essence

Directions

1. Apple purée: Place apples, water and lemon juice in a small pot. Cover and bring to the boil

over a medium heat. Simmer until soft. Drain liquid, but keep it. Purée with a stick blender until smooth and add some of the cooking liquid, if necessary.

2. Muffins: Preheat oven to 180 °C. Place muffin cups into a muffin pan or lightly grease the pan.

3. Mix all the dry ingredients together and stir in the grated apple. Mix the remaining ingredients together.

4. Stir the liquid ingredients into the dry ingredients to form a smooth batter. Take care not to over-mix it. Spoon into muffin cups and bake for 25-30 minutes or until a skewer comes out clean.

5. Cool on a cooling rack. Serve a muffin per person as a snack or in a lunch box.

TIPS

1. Any left-over apple purée can be frozen and used for other baking, or used to sweeten savoury dishes. If preferred, the apple cubes

can be simmered with a cinnamon stick – just remove it before puréeing the apples.

2. Add ⅓ cup (80 ml) dried cranberries or raisins to the muffins, if preferred.

POPCORN

Serves 4

Ready In 15min

Homemade popcorn is such a treat and the ideal lunch box filler. A healthier alternative to shop-bought salty snacks like crisps, at home you can control how much salt and oil is used.

Ingredients

- 1 tsp (5 ml) sunflower oil
- ½ cup (125 ml) popcorn kernels
- ¼ tsp (1,2 ml) salt
- 2 tsp (10 ml) dried mixed herbs, origanum or paprika

Directions

1. Place oil in a large pot with a lid and swirl to coat the base of the pot with the oil.

2. Sprinkle the kernels in an even layer on the base of the pot. Cover with a lid and heat over a medium heat.

3. When the popcorn kernels begin to pop, don't leave the pot unattended. When there is more than 2 seconds between each 'pop', remove the pot from the heat. Do not remove the lid until the popping stops.

4. Mix the salt and herbs or spices and sprinkle over the hot popcorn. Toss through and serve immediately.

TIPS

1. Pack popcorn in your kids' lunch boxes. Keep in an airtight container or a sealable plastic bag.

FRESH FRUIT AND PEANUT BUTTER DIP

Serves 4

Ready In 15min

This peanut butter dip makes snacking on fruit even yummier! The peanut butter adds a slightly sweeter flavour to the yoghurt, making it ideal for those late afternoon munchies.

Ingredients

- 3 tbsp (45 ml) peanut butter
- ½ cup (125 ml) plain low-fat yoghurt
- 4 apples or pear, cut in wedges

Directions

1. Place peanut butter in a bowl and mix until slightly softened. Stir in the yoghurt and mix well until smooth.
2. Serve peanut butter dip with fruit wedges as a mid-afternoon snack. The peanut butter and fruit can help to curb your sweet tooth cravings.

TIPS

1. Make a savoury dip for veggie sticks: Mix ½ cup (125 ml) low-fat cottage cheese with ¼ cup (60 ml) plain low-fat yoghurt and season with lemon juice and black pepper. Add chopped fresh herbs, if preferred.

2. Use any seasonal fruit of your choice to dunk into the dip. This is also a great lunch box filler for kids.

3. Add a pinch of cinnamon or a drop of vanilla essence to the dip for a different flavour.

4. Make sure you use a good quality peanut butter that is lower in salt and sugar.

NAFLD WEIGHT TRACKER

Initial Weight (lb):_______ Initial BMI:_______

5% Total Body Weight Loss:_______ 10% Total Body

Target Weight Loss (lb) :_______

(aim for approx. 1 entry/week) (3 month goal) (6 month goal)

Date Weight (lb) BMI Labs (if/when drawn)

Week 1: Hemoglobin A1c:_______ LDL:_______ HDL:_______ Triglycerides:_______

Week 2:

Week 3:

Week 4:

Week 5:

Week 6:

Week 7:

Week 8:

Week 9:

Week 10:

Week 11:

Week 12: Hemoglobin A1c:_______ LDL:_______ HDL:_______ Triglycerides:_______

Week 13:

Week 14:

Week 15:

Week 16:

Week 17:

Week 18:

Week 19:

Week 20:

Week 21:

Week 22:

Week 23:

Week 24: Hemoglobin A1c:_______ LDL:_______ HDL:_______ Triglycerides:_______

NAFLD PHYSICAL ACTIVITY TRACKER

Week: ____/______/_______   — ____/______/_______

Goals:

____

____

____

____

____

____

Week: ____/______/______   — ____/______/______

Goals:

____

____

____

____

____

____

Date Activity Duration (min) Intensity (indicate with X) Notes

Low:______ Moderate:______ High:______

Low:______ Moderate:______ High:______

Low:______ Moderate:______ High:______

Low:______ Moderate:______ High:______

Low:______ Moderate:______ High:______

PHYSICAL ACTIVITY INTENSITY GUIDE:

• Low Intensity: These activities do not change your heart rate. You can still carry on a normal conversation during the activity. Some examples include walking at a normal pace or stretching/resistance based exercises.

• Moderate Intensity: These activities cause your heart rate to increase. You can talk but not sing during the activity. Some examples include brisk walking, running at a moderate pace, or biking at a moderate pace.

• High Intensity: These activities cause your heart rate to increase a lot. You can only have 3-5 word breathy sentences during the activity. Some examples include rapid power walking, running at a fast pace, swimming or biking at a fast pace. It is important to only exercise at High intensity for shorter periods of time based on your fitness level. Consult with your primary care physician before engaging in high intensity physical activity.

PHYSICAL ACTIVITY DURATION GUIDE

Experts say your goal should be one, or a combination, of these:

• Do some sort of moderate aerobic activity, for at least 2½ hours each week. It is up to you how many days you want to exercise, but it is best to be active at least 3 days a week. Be active for at least 10 minutes at a time.

• Or do more vigorous activities, for at least 1¼ hours a week. You can spread out these 75 minutes any way you want to. It is better to be active at least 3 days a week for at least 10 minutes at a time.